THE LABYRINTH

GORDON BOSTIC

PRIMIX
PUBLISHING
THE WRITE CHOICE

Primix Publishing
East Brunswick Office Evolution
1 Tower Center Boulevard, Ste 1510
East Brunswick, NJ 08816
www.primixpublishing.com
Phone: 1-800-538-5788

Published by Primix Publishing: 12/05/2024

ISBN: 979-8-88703-418-8(sc)
ISBN: 979-8-88703-419-5(e)

Library of Congress Control Number: 2024917437

Dedication

In loving memory of my brother Jon.

Contents

Prolog

In poverty his fam'ly mired
Where all hope had been lost.
They had been living day to day
Though barely bore the cost.

Lee had a daughter and a son
That on him had relied.
His wife said they'd be homeless, too,
If he went off and died.

Lee's wife had vowed to stand by him
Through good times and through bad.
And though their fortune had been lost
She was glad that she had.

Lee's wife's name had been Kimberly
Who'd stood through thick and thin.
A woman who had not complained
About the fix they're in.

There'd been one tiny ray of hope
Lee feared beyond his reach.
There was a treasure to pursue
If Labyrinth he'd breach.

There was a fee that was required
Before attempt was made.
It was an opportunity
In which he could be paid.

Though Lee was close to destitute,
He came up with the fee.
His family knew poverty
From which he wished to free.

The Economic Downturn

In the economic downturn
Was when it all began.
Where unemployment reached new heights
And there had been no plan.

The streets teemed with social unrest
As hunger grew widespread.
The people blamed the government
For why they were not fed.

The times were truly desperate
Where hope had given way
To a new sense of hopelessness
That faced them ev'ry day.

It was in that environment
The Labyrinth was born.
To fill the masses with some hope
That would divert the scorn.

The Labyrinth designed to tempt
An end to all their woes.
A carrot placed upon a stick
Whose challenge many chose.

The country clearly in decline
Which had been by design.
The Labyrinth was just a ploy
So, guilt they'd not assign.

Lee's Story

He'd not always been destitute.
It slowly came with time.
A victim of a market place
That was not worth a dime.

It seemed decisions that were made
Were faulty at their core.
So, he, like many others, were
Not wealthy any more.

The country wrapped in lethargy
As most had lost the will
To chase the dreams that they once dreamed
They knew they could not fill.

Though Kim had begged him not to go,
No other choice he'd seen.
The squalor that they'd come to know
He thought had been obscene.

For Kim had meant the world to him
And reason he agreed.
Lee thought that Kim deserved better
Than living life in need.

Where the challenge he'd accepted
With hope he could restore
The life they were entitled to
Which they'd found was no more.

Almost ev'rything he'd worked for
He'd found taken away.
The government had blocked success
And saw no other way.

The governmental handouts
On which they had relied
Had robbed him of his dignity
And took away his pride.

The Government

While the economic downturn
Had put them all at risk.
The government oblivious
Where spending remained brisk.

With soaring prices food grew scarce
And fam'lies hard to feed.
The government made promises
But then ignored the need.

The job market had all dried up
As businesses had moved.
The tax burdens they had incurred
The government approved.

For taxes had been raised so high
Most companies had fled.
Which had only left the people
The government next bled.

The taxes made impossible
For any to succeed.
It could have offered some relief
But had not seen the need.

The government had been at fault
Which no one dared to say.
For all that chose to speak of it
Had simply gone away.

The freedoms that were granted them
Too often were ignored.
While questions that were asked of it
Too often unexplored.

The government had felt their pain
Or so had been its claim.
Its people mired in poverty
While they held it to blame.

They were pawns for its amusement
To do with as it willed.
Its promises, magnanimcus,
Went mostly unfulfilled.

Its mantra was that all was well
Despite how people fared.
As a clear indication of
How little it had cared.

The Challenge

The Labyrinth had been a thought
The government devised.
In hope to quell the discontent
Though purpose it disguised.

The first one who could solve the maze
Would be who claimed the prize
The government claimed lucrative
And worthy of the wise.

It said there would be obstacles
And puzzles to be solved.
There would be risks that must be faced
For those who were involved.

It was designed to prove the point
The government had cared.
Though people's lives had been destroyed
Through policies it dared.

The event it called the Challenge
Which would be televised.
In order to raise revenue
That can't be compromised.

The Challenge that was offered them
Was meant to give them hope
Against a failed economy
That had been huge in scope.

The government would meet their needs
Till fortunes turned around.
Where the Challenge was the device
To which its promise bound.

For the tax base had been reduced
And funds were running low.
To support its lavish lifestyles
It clearly needed doe.

The Challenge, thus, had offered it
The chance to coffers fill.
By offering the populace
A dream they could fulfill.

What happens in the Labyrinth
Would then be up to them.
They could either rise above it
Or devolve and condemn.

The Rules

The panel that ruled the event
Was who had set the rules.
Though some had questioned their intent,
They clearly were not fools.

While the rules had been quite simple
And easy to explain.
So, any questions they may have,
They would not entertain

The Labyrinth had one way in
And only one way out.
They said there would be obstacles
With which they'd have to bout.

They could choose to work together
Or go at it alone.
For once inside the Labyrinth
They would be on their own.

But in the end, those who emerged
Would claim part of the prize.
Which would only be awarded
The ones who proved most wise.

The Reward

The reward was so enticing
There're few who'd hesitate
To undertake the challenge
Unmindful of their fate.

The reward they were offering
Had been beyond belief
For those who're mired in poverty
Would find it a relief.

Where even the smallest portion
Most thought was worth the risk.
The times were truly desperate
With applications brisk.

Although none of the applicants
Had thought the whole thing through.
Some thought there must be more to it
Than any of them knew.

The Challengers

There were one hundred challengers
Who each had sought the prize.
All felt the challenge worth the risk
Which none would compromise.

They all had gathered in small groups
Where dreams they gladly shared.
They had a chance to change their lives
And for that chance they dared.

And each one of the challengers
The labyrinth would face.
None anticipated danger
Once they're inside the place

They gathered on the night before
With each yet to check-in.
Where all prayed for deliverance
From life as it had been.

They, too, had lived in poverty
With no hope of escape.
This was a chance to change their lives
And cease to have to scrape.

Lee asked if any had a plan
For how they should proceed.
But most feared to cooperate
As they'd not seen the need.

The world they knew was dog eat dog
With trust in short supply.
For no one ever offered aid
On which they could rely.

The Rumors

The rumors of the Labyrinth
Served to stir some unrest.
Though little had been known of it
Some workers had confessed.

The Labyrinth was boobytrapped,
Or so the rumors said.
For clearly it was by design
That many would be dead.

Though there'd been little evidence
The rumors had been true.
The Challenge cloaked in secrecy
Where no truth had leaked through.

Though little known of the Challenge
Which seemed done by design.
Where rumors that surrounded it
Forced many to decline.

Perhaps the rumors purposeful
In who they would select.
For it seemed the ones most likely
Knew not what to expect.

A Matter of Concern

When Lee noticed that a young girl
Sat by herself, alone.
Where there're few females in the group
As far as he had known.

At first it seemed she'd been too young
For panel to accept.
As there'd been an age restriction
It seemed she'd barely leapt.

He left his group to go to her
Though he had been ignored.
It seemed she valued privacy
Or presence had abhorred.

Although the fact she's well-endowed
Had led her to believe
Men were never to be trusted
As each one made her grieve.

She'd always been objectified
Thus, always was on guard.
In her past, some took liberties
Which had turned her heart hard.

Perhaps she feared he'd hit on her
Which had not been the case.
He only was concerned for her
With what they were to face.

Lee thought she was too young for this
With risks she'd have to take.
But she refused to speak with him
Even if for her sake.

He was a father, after all,
And she had seemed so young.
Of course, he was concerned for her
But he had held his tongue.

You can lead a horse to water
But cannot make it drink.
While you can advise your children
You cannot make them think.

An Eclectic Group

It would be an eclectic group
With which he would compete.
For they all possessed a story,
Though some were incomplete.

The priest competing for his church
Which on hard times had fell.
Where it was facing bankruptcy
If he should somehow fail.

Jake had once been an accountant
Whose practice slowly died.
Due to a slowed economy
With few assets to hide.

The prostitute had as her goal
To be rid of the life.
She had other aspirations
Among which be a wife.

Though Conner was a humble man,
A hard life all he knew.
Who thought the world deprived him of
The life that he was due.

Gil Peters was a carpenter
Though work grew to be rare.
His mother had been very ill
And needed special care.

Neal Hanson was a laborer
Who for years found no work.
Where he survived on charity
Which made him feel a jerk.

The others' stories much the same
As desperation ruled.
They all had wished a second chance
Where life could be retooled.

Lee's Dream

That night Lee dreamed he'd won the prize
And by the rest was cheered.
It seemed he had a special sense
That through the maze had steered.

He had avoided obstacles
That had been meant to kill.
While ev'ryone had looked to him
With mission to fulfill.

They hailed him as the champion
The minute he emerged.
The maze had been a mystery
But one that he had purged.

His wife and children greeted him
Like they'd not done before.
As though he was a warrior
Who just returned from war.

Then from his dream when Lee awoke
He saw it was not real.
Although the dream had left him with
A very eerie feel.

Kim's Reservations

Although Kim had reservations
She also must admit
The faith that she had placed in him
Had always proved legit.

For family he'd sacrificed
Like none should have to do.
While her faith in him rewarded
By what they had been through.

She understood his reasoning
Though she had disagreed.
The risks she thought had been too great
Where she'd not seen the need.

While their lives had not been perfect
They had, so far, made do.
So, this had seemed a reckless act
He'd no need to see through.

He was ashamed of the handouts
By which they had survived.
As unemployment ruled the land
Where pride he'd been deprived.

The pressures he had come to feel
She knew had hit him hard.
But this was outright foolishness
She wished he'd disregard.

Check-in

They all were sworn to secrecy
Where they could not reveal
The secrets of the Labyrinth
Which was part of the deal.

There had also been disclaimers
Each entrant had to sign.
The task was more than arduous
As lives were on the line.

Lee wondered why non-disclosures
They said must be obtained.
There was no need for secrecy
If all could be explained.

So, if any of the rumors
Had proven to be true.
There's no one who could verify
As no one had a clue.

The fees with which they had to part
Had proven to be high.
Especially for those of them
That barely could scrape by.

There was a special area
To where they were assigned.
Where families were not allowed
But challengers confined.

Kim held and kissed him long and hard
Till Lee was led away.
Kim screamed that she would pray to God
That he would be okay.

Gil

There was a member of the group
Val found she did not trust.
Gil seemed to be a sleazy guy
Who's look was one of lust.

He was extremely arrogant
And over confident.
He, too, was argumentative
Who always voiced dissent.

She found him brazen with his boasts
Though pretty sure he lied.
To her he had not seemed the type
Where courage had applied.

The Challenge not yet underway,
Yet, threat he clearly posed.
She thought Gil an opportunist
That was not, yet, exposed.

He thought that he had been a catch
But Val had thought no way.
For she knew if she had caught him
He's one she'd toss away.

The Labyrinth

The labyrinth had proved more vast
Than Lee, at first, believed.
While the challenge he'd accepted
He now thought ill conceived.

Its walls had seemed to touch heaven,
At least twenty feet tall.
The structure was magnificent
And towered over all.

The doors were massive in design
Though no windows in view.
It had looked more like a fortress
Than a gameshow venue.

Lee got an uneasy feeling
As Labyrinth he'd view.
He thought there must be more to this
Than any of them knew.

Valerie

Lee saw the girl was fidgety
But when he turned to speak
She merely rolled her eyes at him
As wisdom she'd not seek.

Lee told her he was nervous too
Where her attention gained.
Many questions were unanswered
Or poorly were explained.

She said her name was Valerie,
But most had called her Val.
Because her fam'ly indigent
Which Lee had thought banal.

She was her fam'ly's only hope
To escape poverty.
But as she stood outside its walls
She feared her destiny.

Entry to the Labyrinth

They gathered at the starting line
Where nervousness had reigned.
Some tried to exude confidence
But Lee had thought it feigned.

Where most were pretty confident
They knew what was in store.
As all had seen the TV show
And needed nothing more.

Lee's rationale had been concise:
Nothing in life is free.
There must be more to the challenge
Than what the eyes could see.

Then as the door was flung open
Into the dark they'd dash.
Unsuspecting of the dangers
Where many acted rash.

Though Lee had not been one of them
As he'd not seen the need.
There could be dangers ev'rywhere
So, caution he would heed.

Then as the last one entered in
The doors had slammed shut tight,
So, now there was no turning back
Nor any chance of flight.

They all had felt a sense of doom
Once the door had been closed.
Who knew what truly lurked within
To which they'd be exposed?

The government's assurances
Had left an eerie feel.
For none of them were confident
The truth it would reveal.

Then Lee told Val to stick with him
And not rush off alone.
He feared there had been more to this
Than he or she had known.

Once the labyrinth was entered
Their fate was clearly sealed.
There only was one exit point
That's said to be concealed.

The first thing that Lee had noticed
How peaceful it had seemed.
There had been no indication
With what inside had teemed.

The labyrinth was dimly lit
Which made it hard to see
What obstacles awaited them
With complete clarity.

As Lee watched his competitors
Run reckless though the halls.
He thought they'd made a huge mistake
As they ignored the walls.

The Flash of Light

Lee warned them not to blindly run
Down any murky hall.
The Labyrinth was dimly lit
Where they could trip and fall.

Although greed was an ncentive
That could not be contained.
So, some took off like maniacs
Who could not be restrained.

The greedy ones the first to die
Who'd chosen not to think.
The prize was all they cared about
Which drove them to the brink.

The flash of light had been blinding
That preceded the screams.
As walls erupted into flames
Erasing wealthy dreams.

In panic they had tried to run
Which only fed the flames.
The others stood in total shock
Grown wary of the claims.

Lee, fearlessly, had taken charge
And rushed to those on fire.
He ripped his shirt off in attempt
The flames he could retire.

But all his efforts were in vain
As they were too far gone.
The rest had merely stood and watched
As eyes were to him drawn.

The rest had frozen in their tracks
With what they saw occur.
This went beyond what they'd been told
Where doubts began to stir.

While their screams had been horrific
There's nothing they could do
Except to watch their agony
Until their screams were through.

They could not even mourn for them
As they'd not known their names.
They were faceless competitors
Who thought they're playing games.

Lee turned to Val and saw the shock
That streamed across her face.
She'd seen the stark reality
That now defiled the place.

He prayed he could return to Kim
But chances now seemed slim.
He'd rejected all Kim's warnings
So, guilt had laid with him.

Some raced back towards the entryway
In effort to escape.
As they'd lost int'rest in the prize
And goals chose to reshape.

No other option left to them
They had to forge ahead.
Although it had been clear to most
That most would soon be dead.

Val's Admiration

Val had masked her admiration
As she bandaged Lee's hands.
Because the courage he displayed
She thought respect demands.

She'd never met someone like Lee
Who'd proven to be brave.
As most men that she'd encountered
Were little more than knave.

While she'd felt a strong attraction
He'd been a mystery.
As she'd no way of knowing him
Beyond what she could see.

And, yet, she'd found him intriguing
Just knowing what she knew.
He seemed to be of hero stock
Whose heart was good and true.

After the Flames

After the flames, their progress slowed,
As caution was employed.
For none had known with certainty
What other traps deployed.

There had been some indecision
On what they next should do.
For the shock of the occurrence
Had shook them through and through.

With dead ends often boobytrapped,
Death came as a surprise.
Where recklessness that some had shown
Had proved to be unwise.

As always there had been the few
Who had refused to heed
The good advice they gave to them
So great had been their greed.

Instead, they raced down dim lit halls
Oblivious to fear.
Who still believed what they'd been told
As reason they were here.

The screams and pleas of those dying
Had echoed through the halls.
But none had dared to go to them
For what hid in the walls.

Their dreams had turned into nightmares
That they could not escape.
Though they'd expected obstacles
That's not the true landscape.

The Path He'd Chosen

Kim hated the path he'd chosen
Believing risk too great.
They did not live an easy life
But Lee was tempting fate.

They may not have a wealth of things
But love had filled their lives.
At times it had been difficult
Though found their love still thrives.

But Lee, Kim feared, had risked it all
In effort to improve
What he believed their lot in life
Of which he'd disapprove.

Kim hated the path he'd chosen
As she had greatly feared
That the outcome of the Challenge
Already engineered.

No Sense of Relief

Though they'd proceeded with caution,
They'd no sense of relief.
While it's said there's strength in numbers,
It was a false belief.

As spikes exploded from the walls
Where eight of them were speared.
While half had been killed instantly.
The others, death had neared.

Val was the first to go to them
Despite a threat remained.
For they'd no way too know for sure
If safety was attained.

Their wounds had been untreatable
As they lacked expertise.
They each had suffered horribly
As one by one they'd cease.

While Val had done her level best
To ease them through their pain.
Her tears began to freely flow
Though she tried to abstain.

These deaths had hit them very hard
As they'd watched them expire.
The deaths that happened earlier
Were hidden by the fire.

Lee saw that caution's not enough
To help them to the end.
So, he ordered the spears removed
Where reach they could extend.

Too many were caught by surprise
As they'd no way to know
What dangers laid ahead of them
Nor which way they should go.

Lee's Shadow

Since they'd entered the Labyrinth
Val never left his side.
It's clear she'd placed her faith in him
And with him would abide.

He'd told her to stick close to him
Which, clearly, she had done.
For when he walked, she, too, would walk,
And when he'd run, she'd run.

She'd become to him a shadow
Who step for step had matched.
She never questioned what he said
Nor any plan he hatched.

For he exuded confidence
Which she greatly admired.
His courage unmistakable
And with doubt was not mired.

She trusted his intuition
Though she could not say why.
But there'd been something about him
That said he was the guy.

The Gamble

Paul often chose to walk with Lee
As it made Paul feel safe.
He knew their lives in jeopardy
With the Labyrinth unsafe.

Paul noticed Val was glued to Lee
Which had led Paul to think
That Val had known something of Lee
From whom she would not shrink.

Thus, Paul had chosen to stay close
In hope he would survive.
For ev'rything that they'd been through,
Those two remained alive.

Paul thought it more than happenstance
The two had been unscathed.
So, he would toss his lot with them
And in their light he bathed.

While Paul not much of a gambler
The odds he thought were clear.
Either Lee was very lucky
Or fate had held him dear.

Daddy's a Celebrity

When their children had come to her
To ask where daddy's gone.
She had no recourse but explain
The mission he was on.

Although unsure they'd understood
Their fears, for now, allayed.
Kim only wished she had believed
That they'd not been betrayed.

They'd watched the progress that he'd
made
In front of their TV.
Not knowing that reality
Was not what they would see.

They thought he's a celebrity
Where they had been enthralled.
As they'd watched daddy on TV
While their mom was appalled.

There was something with the broadcast
That had not appeared right.
The people seemed superimposed
To manufactured site.

But the scene brought Kim to worry
The Challenge was a lie.
And she believed it's lies they'd shown
Though she had not kncwn why.

The Fountains

There was no food provided them
Though fountains were in place.
But there were few who chose to drink
With death no wish to face.

Most feared the fountains were a trap
That had been poison laced.
While thirst became a constant need
They desperately faced.

But most would rather die from thirst
Than dare to take a drink.
It mattered not if true or false,
But what they'd come to think

It was the biggest travesty
The Labyrinth had housed.
Salvation could have been at hand
If truth had been espoused.

A Primal Force

Lee saw in Val a primal force
That could not be denied.
For she'd shown determination
Her appearance belied.

Perhaps more credit she deserved
For courage she displayed.
While she, clearly, was not reckless
She functioned while afraid.

Her spirit undeniable
As she refused to quit.
Although she, too, could be headstrong
To panic not submit.

She had ignored adversity
And first to offer aid.
She was someone they could count on
Even if she's afraid.

She reminded Lee of Kimberly
In all too many ways.
Whom he hoped to soon return to
Depending how this plays.

The Fee

Lee had wondered to himself
Why had they charged a fee?
When it had claimed to help the poor
Escape their poverty.

He thought there was a disconnect
Between what's claimed and true.
He wished that he had thought of this
Before his fee came due.

Val could see that Lee was thinking
As he seemed far away.
But when she asked him for his thoughts
Lee had refused to say.

But Val refused to let it go
As she had grown concerned.
For whatever he was thinking
His visage clearly turned.

Reluctantly, Lee said to Val
What really puzzled him.
What was the purpose of the fee
That had been charged to them?

A Lack of Focus

Though Lee wanted to stay focused,
He found his mind would stray.
His thoughts would turn to Kimberly
And prayed she was okay.

His children, too, would cross his mind,
For whom he greatly cared.
It was only for their welfare
The Challenge he had cared.

But Kimberly had been his life
Who he would not betray,
He'd given her his heart and soul
Which he'd not throw away.

He swore that he would stand by Kim
As she would stand by him.
Their love was more than physical
That bonded both of them.

Lee hoped that Kim was confident
Whatever may befall.
He always would be there for her
And giving it his all.

Paul's Demise

Each step was taken warily
As with each step they'd fear
Another opportunity
For death to interfere.

When Paul had wandered off the path
They screamed for his return.
Too many lives already lost
Of those who failed to learn.

A rod that had embedded spikes
Next pinned Paul to the wall.
While the others had ignored him
Lee stopped to help Paul.

While Paul in fear reached out to Lee,
It's Val who took his hand.
As Lee tried to remove the rod,
Val's comforting was grand.

But Paul, it seemed, already dead
With other deaths to come.
The labyrinth was a death trap
They could not overcome.

Val Took Lee's Hand

When Val had softly grabbed his hand
It caught Lee by surprise.
He found the gesture dangerous
In what she may surmise.

He feared she had designs on him
Which never could come true.
For Lee already had a wife
He hoped to go home to.

He thought, perhaps, their brush with death
Had sparked some inner need.
That had required another's touch
Where fear she'd not concede.

Perhaps it was assurances
That she had sought to find.
A need to know she's not alone
And put at ease her mind.

Perhaps it's a father figure
That Val had really sought.
For Lee was nearly twice her age
And she had seemed distraught.

Although when Lee had pulled away
The look that claimed Val's face
Had been one of disappointment
That Lee could not embrace.

There'd be no infidelity
As far as Lee's concerned.
No matter what she offered him
His heart could not be turned.

The Whisperers

Val saw the groups of whisperers
And wondered what was said.
The sudden trends of secrecy
She had begun to dread.

It's Gil who chose to instigate
What Val thought a revolt.
The accusations that Gil made
Had, truly, been a jolt.

It's the ultimate betrayal
Lee would be forced to face.
He already was guilt ridden,
Now he they'd wish replace.

Val feared it's a conspiracy
To do away with Lee.
For Gil had been a hardened man
Who's prone to jealousy.

Gil claimed under Lee's leadership
That all they'd known was death.
Although, perhaps, what was the truth
The reason they drew breath.

The things that Gil accused Lee of
Had, clearly, not been true.
Though a multitude persuaded
No loyalty Lee's due.

While Val feared the implications
There's little she could do.
Their fear had made them gullible
Which Gil already knew.

Gil saw he had an opening
To play upon their fear.
Where it had been a power grab
That he would engineer.

They still were smarting from the shock
Where their comrades had died.
Gil claimed that some could have been saved
But Lee had never tried.

The Lynchpin

When Val had seen Lee's look had changed,
She asked what he had thought.
For this far they'd made together
Where death they'd not yet bought.

In horror it occurred to Lee
The Challenge was a lie.
For ev'rything they'd seen so far
Had shown they're meant to die.

Where Lee now feared with certainty
No exit would exist.
The panic that had gripped his heart,
He found hard to resist.

The awful truth he had to face;
There never was a prize.
Just those lured through desperation
Which proved to be unwise.

Then Val had simply stared at him
As though in disbelief.
For it's he who was the lynchpin
That fueled the rest's belief.

An Object of Desire

Inside they lost all track of time
So, had no way to know.
How long they'd been confined inside
Nor how far yet to go.

When Lee felt safety had been reached
He told the others, rest.
They had no clue to what's ahead
As they pursued their quest.

That night Val laid down next to him
Which had raised an alarm.
Her wish to be familiar,
Though not without its charm.

He must admit he was flattered
As object of desire.
Although it's of no consequence
For he'd not felt the fire

But the vow that he had taken
He swore he would not breach.
He believed what Val was seeking
Had laid beyond her reach.

The Snake Pit

The floor had simply given way
Where those who'd took the lead
Had simply disappeared from sight
As though some trap was keyed.

What had remained an open pit
Into which seven fell.
Where their screams had been bloodcurdling
As though they'd entered hell.

Lee and two others ran to them
In hope that they could save
The ones who fell into the pit
Which soon would be their grave.

The pit was filled with deadly snakes
Which was a ghastly sight.
While they screamed for deliverance
They were left to their plight.

They found the pit had been too deep
To execute rescue.
So, helplessly, they'd only watched
As their deaths had come due.

A narrow ledge on either side
They cautiously employed
To work their way around the pit
Which none of them enjoyed.

The spears they use for balancing
So narrow was the ledge.
Where they had hoped if someone slipped
They'd pull them to the edge.

When all had passed but Val and Lee,
They found when came their turn
The footing was more treacherous
Than they'd at first discern.

For Val had slipped and nearly fell
Where by the spear was held.
Her screams had reflected terror
For what beneath her welled.

When Val was rescued from the pit
She quickly embraced Lee.
Though he had played no part in it
Which was a mystery.

To Find They Were Misled

Lee stood before those who remained
To claim they'd been misled.
The challenge of the Labyrinth
Had left too many dead.

Lee knew he must accept the fact
That on him they relied.
Survival, now, their only goal
And he they chose to guide.

The Challenge seemed a penalty
That they were meant to pay
For their years of bellyaching
Of living day to day.

While the people lived like paupers,
Those who ruled lived like kings.
Who took advantage of despair
To become wealthy beings.

They had no knowledge of remorse
As they had never cared.
The hardships brought by policies
That deemed how people fared.

It seemed that what was televised
Was clearly less than true.
The Labyrinth more dangerous
Than any of them knew.

Trust Issues

The truce that they had first enjoyed
Slowly began to fade.
As the body count had mounted
And they'd grown more afraid.

Alliances that once were strong
Had become slightly frayed.
Were all were, now, in jeopardy
As trust issues were weighed

Perhaps, because Gil stirred the pot
The issues had arose.
For he'd clearly been divisive
In what he would propose.

They then turned on one another
As accusations flew.
Where all had felt they were exposed
To any who're in view.

Too many at each other's throats
As death threats had been made.
Where it's more than the Labyrinth
Of which they were afraid.

Their only goal had come to be
An effort to survive.
For many had come to believe
That few would leave a ive.

Their lives degraded to the point
Where most had ceased to care
If, truly, there had been a prize
That had been worth the dare.

The Temptation

The moment Val came onto him
Lee tried to push aside
The temptation that he had felt
And tried so hard to hide.

The way that Val came onto him
Had left Lee little doubt
What were truly Val's intentions
And what she was about.

He saw the signs were clearly there
The way she'd primp and preen.
Though actions he tried to ignore,
The invitation seen.

Each step they took could be their last
So, what had he to lose?
The chance that he'd see Kim again
Was slim, he'd come to muse.

Besides, there was the loneliness
With which they must contend.
It was a chance to touch someone
Before he met his end.

The Feeling

The feeling that came over Kim
Had told her something's wrong.
Though the feeling she'd not pinpoint
It truly had been strong.

She knew that Lee had faced a threat
Though had no true detail.
She feared the Challenge was a ruse
Where all were meant to fail.

She wished that she could go to him
But that was not allowed.
For now, she had to bide her time
And hope he'd not been bowed.

Though the feeling left her queasy,
Surrender not her way.
Until she was told otherwise
She'd assume Lee's okay.

Like Family

The situation they were in
Had served to build a bond.
Where they'd become like family;
Perhaps, a bit beyond.

Each step they took was compromised
Which placed on them a strain.
With seeds of discord quick to grow
Which quickly became plain.

The family that they'd become
Began to slowly fray.
As pressure from the Labyrinth
Began to on them weigh.

Many thought that Lee betrayed them
Where he had seen the pit.
But had not uttered a warning
He was aware of it.

Which led to death of seven more
Who did not have to die.
Where they all began to question
As to the reason why.

Though Val had claimed it was not true.
For how was Lee to know?
They'd no map of the Labyrinth
That said which way to go.

That's When They Chose to Separate

And go their diff'rent ways.
Believing if they're rid of Lee,
Longer would be their days.

Gil called them a band of rebels
Who'd see the journey through.
He'd lead them to the promised land
As Moses tried to do.

Gil tossed a sly smile right at Lee
As though he'd somehow won
A contest within a contest
That Lee thought far from done.

A Husband and a Father

Kim found her dreams would turn to him
The few times she could sleep.
For worry kept her up at night
For her love had run deep.

Although her warnings he ignored
She knew it was because
He thought he could deliver them
Which had become his cause.

As a husband and a father
Lee felt it's up to him
To provide for his family
And to be there for them.

But circumstances had been such
The choice had not been his.
For the economic downturn
Had took away his biz.

Unable to find employment,
He felt that he had failed.
He now believed he was a drain
As his life was derailed.

So, his entry to the Challenge
A way of saving face.
Even if the Challenge killed him
He'd not be a disgrace.

A Gruesome Spectacle

The hall had looked innocuous
As their entry was made.
When a sound caught their attention
That left them all afraid.

The ones the closest to the edge
Were able to race free.
But those on the interior
Had not been as lucky.

The walls were closing in on them
Though they had tried to run.
Pure panic had a grip on them
In knowledge they were done.

The walls were like a juggernaut
That could not be restrained.
While their screams had been heart wrenching,
Where fear was unconstrained.

But when the walls had been recalled
A ghastly sight revealed.
Their bodies were completely crushed
For which they'd not been steeled

The sight had made some very ill
As it was hard to see.
It was a gruesome spectacle
From which they could not flee.

As they had moved away from it,
Some still were pretty ill.
The image still had haunted them
And feared it always will.

Her Children's Questions

Kim's children asked her constantly
When daddy would return.
But Kim was at a loss for words
And knew not where to turn.

Her children, clearly, were too young
For Challenge to accept.
So, how could she explain to them
The reasons that she wept.

It almost broke her heart to see
The questioning they'd shown.
Although she knew they had no clue
To fears that she had known.

For them their father risked his life
In hope he could provide
The life that he had wished for them
But that he'd not confide.

Her children asked where daddy went
But what was she to say?
He'd left to risk his life for them
And try to save the day?

She wished she had a stock answer
That she could just repeat.
But she had questions of her own
With no answer to greet.

She understood his reasoning
But for it did not care.
Her children deserved a father
Who always would be there.

The Pressure

The pressure that they'd been under
On some began to wear.
Where they'd begun to strangely act
And greater risks would dare.

Where some committed suicide
Which had not been that hard.
For all they really had to do
Was safety disregard.

While others seemed to lose their minds
As though they'd gone insane.
Where they would pick a corridor
With freedom to attain.

While they all had faced exhaustion
And escape thoughts had dimmed.
They had little other options
As threads of hope were trimmed.

There were signs of desperation
As recklessness was shown.
The caution that had once prevailed
Had to the wind been thrown.

For death awaited any who
Would dare let down their guard.
The Labyrinth the arbiter
Whose judgment harsh and hard.

Josh Perkins

Josh Perkins was a case in point
Who simply disappeared.
One moment he was with the group,
The next moment he veered.

Though no one knew where Josh had gone,
The rumors had run wild.
Some claimed that he had gone insane
As he had run hog-wild.

His laugh would echo through the halls
Which left an eerie feel.
Though how he managed to survive
Had almost seemed surreal.

The fact that Josh had not yet died
Had raised questions galore.
For the many who were cautious
Had been killed by the score.

They never knew where Josh may be
But judging from the sound
It seemed that Josh had owned the place
The way he got around.

The Stench

The stench became unbearable
From rotting and decay.
The bodies of those who'd been killed
Were left just where they'd lay.

For inside of the Labyrinth
The air already stale.
Where the bodies of the fallen
Made it hard to inhale.

From cloth they crudely fashioned masks
Though offered little aid.
As the smell was penetrating
And in the air had laid.

While the stench was overwhelming
They'd no choice but move on.
As the smell would only worsen
Was the conclusion drawn.

A Hail of Darts

The hail of darts that showered them
Had come from ev'rywhere.
Where some were struck with multiples
As they fell from the air.

A dart had caught Lee in the arm
And it had hurt like hell.
But there were others worse than he
Who had not fared as well.

Lee was amazed Val was not hit
The way the darts had rained.
It seemed she was the only one
No injury sustained.

Though true Lee had tried to shield her
He, too, had been amazed.
Not a single dart had struck her
To where she'd not been grazed.

While Lee found in protecting her
As though she was his child.
It had put them both in danger
As choices made were wild.

As Val had pulled the dart from Lee
The blood began to flow.
It lodged much deeper than she thought
And almost laid him low.

Val worried that they were poisoned
Where those who're hit would die.
And she'd be left in solitude
Which made her start to cry.

Lee found his heart went out to her
To see her in that light.
For despite what she intended
He had felt for her plight.

Lee thought it was unfair to judge
For he, too, was afraid.
Whatever Val wished to pursue
She would not be waylaid.

Val said another ten were dead
And some injured severe.
She's sure there're some who could not walk
Or so, it would appear.

Lee had a choice he had to make
Which left him less than thrilled.
For any that were left behind
He may as well have killed.

In an already weakened state
It had been clear to Lee.
There was no way to carry those
Whose death a certainty.

But he felt an obligation
To those who could be saved.
Which would require a sacrifice
Where some lives must be waived.

No Fan of Gil

Val had not been a fan of Gil
And made that very clear.
Where ev'ry time he spoke to her
She'd pretend not to hear.

Gil thought that he had sex appeal
But that Val had not seen.
He thought he was a ladies' man
Though Val found him obscene.

He had twice tried to seduce her
But each attempt for naught.
For the lines he tried to feed her
Were ones Val had not bought.

She thought he was a sleazy guy
She was not prone to trust.
She found she rarely dealt with him
Unless she found she must.

She'd never place her faith in him
As she'd come to believe
His first response to a challenge
Would be try to deceive.

Lee's Injury

Val had feared Lee's arm infected
The way it had turned red.
She believed he needed treatment
Or soon he may be dead.

For when his dressing she had changed
The sight had worried her.
There had been no sign of healing,
At least, she could infer.

Val asked him if his arm had hurt
To which Lee replied no.
She thought that he had lied to her
So, she'd not worry so.

They weren't prepared to do first-aid
And medicine had none.
So, any tiny injury
Could mean that they were done.

They, thus, were forced to improvise
With what they had on-hand.
Where Val's shirt was growing shorter
With ev'ry new armband.

Gil's Band of Rebels

It had not taken very long
To find it had been clear.
Gil had proved to be no leader
As he'd been ruled by fear.

His decisions a disaster
For which they all had paid.
For he'd proven indecisive
In choices that he made.

As ev'ry choice that Gil had made
Had meant someone may die.
Where many had grown hesitant
To dare on him rely.

The water fountain he claimed clean
Had killed nearly a score.
They thought he'd turned his back on them
Where vengeance some had swore.

He led them into boobytraps
He clearly should have seen.
And all the while he claimed that Lee
Was who they should demean.

The ones who chose to follow him
Regretted their mistake.
For those who had been married thought
Gil would a widow make.

They thought that Gil was dangerous
So, they had turned on him,
Where the beating they delivered
Had ripped him limb from limb.

Val's Admission

Val wanted to admit to Lee
The things she'd come to feel.
But recognized the circumstance
May lessen the appeal.

Val feared if she had opened up
To tell him how she felt
That Lee may turn his back on her –
A hand she'd not be dealt.

It could be unrequited love,
For she was not a fool.
But she would never know for sure
If she let silence rule.

When Val had thrown herself at him
It came as no surprise.
Lee saw the signs already there
But would not compromise.

While Lee told her he was flattered
Their love could never be.
For he had been a married man
Who had a family.

Though he had no wish to hurt her,
The facts must be made plain.
Another woman claimed his heart
Was what he tried explain.

Val took the opportunity
To tell Lee how she felt.
While Lee had listened patiently
His heart started to melt.

Val wished to say she'd die for him
But thought what was the use.
Already Lee possessed a wife
Which would be his excuse.

Her admiration for the man
Had led to so much more.
The feelings that she had for him
She wanted to explore.

Although Val's heart had been broken
She refused to deride
The loyalty that she owed Lee,
Thus, could not leave his side.

She promised herself she'd not cry
Though it had become clear
That there had been no hope for them
Which she'd no wish to hear.

Val's feelings she had pushed aside
Though difficult to do.
In the hope that her allegiance
Would help to see her through.

The Dreams

Kimberly had been a fixture
In ev'ry dream Lee dreamed.
But, lately, Val sometimes appeared
Where Lee had woke and screamed.

While Kimberly had claimed his heart,
She was a world away.
While Val was always at his side
And with him ev'ry day.

The dreams had made him hate himself
To think he'd entertain
A possible relationship
Knowing he should refrain.

Had the threat of death so changed him
That he would disavow
Ev'rything that he believed in
For pleasure here and now?

Then thought his mind was playing tricks
In helping him to cope.
Despite how bad it may have seemed,
He'd not surrender hope.

If death should be the end result,
Lee made a solemn vow.
He'd die the man he'd always been
As to fear he'd not bow.

A Threat to Lee

The feelings Kim experienced
At least, one time before.
Once again had overwhelmed her
With what may be in store.

She felt as though Lee faced a threat
That had caught him off guard.
Although Lee had been pragmatic
And fooling him was hard.

So, she'd felt the threat was subtle
And may have been disguised.
For her intuition told her
By it, Lee was surprised.

She'd never questioned loyalty,
As she'd known him so well.
But feared what he was going through
Had been akin to hell.

What's to Come?

While Val felt some disappointment
What also had been true
At least for now she'd be with him.
Where what's to come? Who knew?

For locked within the Labyrinth
No competition loomed.
She still had time to change his mind
Lest either one was doomed.

For Val, the Labyrinth a gift
That she would not return.
This circumstance had brought her Lee
For whom her heart would yearn.

The threat of death had brought them close
But Val had wanted more.
She wanted him to want her too,
As he she did adore.

She had admired his loyalty
But thought it was misplaced.
Because the danger that they shared,
In her, it should be placed.

Although she had not told him so,
What she had most desired
Was claim the heart another owned.
The man she most admired.

While trapped within the Labyrinth
Val knew she'd still a chance
Where she could turn his heart around
And hope for a romance.

Though she knew it sounded crazy
She could not help herself.
He's ev'rything she ever dreamed
And not stuck on himself.

Those Remaining

Where besides Val, were Neal and Jake,
Who chose to stay with Lee.
For they'd not lost their confidence
In Lee's ability.

All thought they lived on borrowed time
Where Lee was their best chance
To make it through the Labyrinth
If not by happenstance.

They could not tell how far they'd come
Nor how far yet to go.
It seemed they're puppets on a string
Condemned to live the show.

As if the Challenge was a tease
To fill them with false hope.
Where all that had been left to them
Was one small strand of rope.

It was Lee who chose direction
His small group would pursue.
Where he believed the opposite
Of what Gil's group would do.

The Adaptation

Lee thought they'd been this way before
Though nothing seemed the same.
As if the walls would somehow shift
To block from whence they came.

And with the shift new obstacles
Were surely put in play.
New dangers that awaited them
That had been meant to slay.

He looked at those who looked to him
Though answers he had none.
If it could rearrange itself
He feared that they were done.

If the Labyrinth adapted
To choices that were made.
There was no way to overcome
The plans that had been laid.

A lifetime spent in wandering
To never find an end.
The irony, the ultimate,
With which they must contend.

Lee never told them what he feared
As he had seen no need.
Whatever was to come of them
Their fear he would not feed.

The Tiled Floor

Unlike the halls already passed
The path ahead was tiled.
The change had been too obvious
Which had left them beguiled.

They could not tell what laid beyond
Nor what the tiles may hide.
But all believed it's certain death
If onto them they'd strice.

Lee noticed Neil still held a spear
Which he asked Neil pass him.
Though it was a crazy rotion,
It had not been a whim.

Then Lee slowly approached the tiles
Where spear Lee chose extend.
He told the rest to stay behind
As with tiles he'd contend.

The spear Lee pushed across the tiles
Half expecting a bomb.
Then swung the spear from side to side
As sweaty grew his palm.

He worked his way across the floor
Thinking he soon may die.
Until he reached the other side
Where he let out a sigh.

Val swore that she'd not dared to breathe
While Lee had made his sweep.
Where his death she half expected
To leave him in a heap.

Lee told them when they crossed the floor
To follow in his steps.
For there had been no guarantee
What happens with missteps.

Then one by one they crossed the floor
The same way Lee had done.
Although their sense of confidence
Was truly close to none.8

As each completed their crossing,
They each breathed in relief
Then each of them gave thanks to Lee
Though hid their disbelief.

Val ran and leaped into Lee's arms
And then gave him a hug.
It seemed she looked for a response
But all Lee did was shrug.

The Final Straw

A row of crossbows rigged to fire
If threshold should be crossed
Both Neal and Jake in line of fire
Where both their lives were lost.

In the horror of the moment
They'd both began to cry.
Their limits had almost been reached
With both prepared to die.

Lee's composure had been shaken.
Perhaps the others right.
Perhaps he was the focal point
That had enhanced their plight.

It seemed disaster followed him
Or to it he would lead.
Too many who'd believed in him
Had died due to the need.

The deaths began to we gh on him
Where he thought he's at fault.
They had followed his direction
And death he'd failed to halt.

Lee felt it was the final straw
As he could take no more.
The evil that consumed the place
had clearly upped the score.

Val saw the guilt that Lee had felt
Was strewn across his face.
The deaths were not because of him
But were due to this place.

Val remarked that the body count
Was not because of him.
Despite the guilt that he had felt
He'd still saved both of them.

For the first time Lee looked at her
And with the look had seen
It was true beauty Val possessed
Which he had failed to glean.

The Reunion

Two tunnels merged into a hall
Where exit door they spied.
With the two groups reunited
But still were not allied.

There were only six survivors
And two in a bad way.
While there had been no sign of Gil
As if he'd stayed away.

Beneath his breath, Lee asked for Gil
But that was when they said
Gil walked into a boobytrap
Where, now, poor Gil was dead.

Good riddance Val had wished to say
But she had held her tongue.
For that may only make things worse
With more barbs to be flung.

The Announcement

When Kim had heard the announcement
The Challenge almost done
She had bundled up their children
In hope that Lee had won.

They gathered with the families
Of those the Challenge dared.
All wondering who would emerge
And how their loved ones fared.

But the crowd had grown impatient
That the door remained closed.
Authorities had grown concerned
The crowd a threat had posed.

For it had grown belligerent
In face of its unrest.
Thinking those in the Labyrinth
Had surely passed the test

Although when the door had opened
A hush fell on the crowd.
The few stragglers who had emerged
Had brought to hope a cloud.

The sobs and cries had been intense
While Kim had been relieved.
For of the three who staggered out
She saw Lee was reprieved.

Lee collapsed in his exhaustion
Believing he was done.
While others had stepped over him,
Continuing to run.

The injured two were left behind
Without a second thought.
Where they succumbed to injuries
The Labyrinth had wrought.

Kim ran to him as Lee collapsed
Afraid he may be hurt.
But overjoyed he was alive
And facing a rebirth.

The Exit from the Labyrinth

They waited for the door to lift
Where they'd, at last, be free.
And the nightmare would be over
As far as they could see.

Val knew love was impossible
As Lee had told her so.
But found she could not help herself
As she could not let go.

Perhaps if she could reach his wife
Before Lee got to her.
The threat she would eliminate
Even if it's murder.

As the exit door had opened,
Val took off on the run.
It was the chance for Val's escape
And with this nightmare done.

Although Lee had tried to grab her
He only grasped thin air.
He next tried calling out to her,
To warn her to beware.

A pit then opened under Val
Into which she had fell.
Lee hoped he'd find she was okay
As he rushed to the wel .

He found her body was impaled
Which had not been deserved.
Her death had been a travesty
Which had left Lee unnerved.

Though he wished to claim her body
The pit had been too deep.
Except for the protruding spikes
She looked to be asleep.

Lee screamed his curses to its walls
As he slumped to his krees.
How could Val's death be justified
The essence of his pleas.

Lee admitted it's resentment
That he had come to feel
This had never been a contest
Though it was all too real.

As Lee stared at her dead body
He wondered what's the point.
For the level of the cruelty
Had been hard to pinpoint.

As there seemed to be no purpose
Except torture and kill.
For reasons had eluded him
What they meant to fulfill.

Like the others, Val was murdered
Which to him made no sense.
For he could not see a purpose
As she had no defense.

He took off running recklessly
Accepting of his fate.
Where now assured that his reward
Was linked to heaven's gate.

The sunlight nearly blinded him
As he crossed through the door.
He cared not what awaited him
As he could take no more.

The Aftermath

Government representatives
The crowd had next addressed.
Who said there'd been some accidents.
Condolences expressed.

But the crowd had grown unruly
So deep had been their grief.
Where it had blamed the government
Who offered no relief.

The families of those who died
Were allowed to retrieve
The remains of their departed
Over which they could grieve.

Their bodies placed in body bags
With just their heads exposed.
So, they could be identified
Though death cause und sclosed.

While Kim and Lee hugged each other
An agent approached Lee.
Who had held a piece of paper
He wished for Lee to see.

It had been his non-disclosure
The agent had in hand.
If ever Lee chose to disclose
He had to understand

The penalty that he would face
Would be more than a fine.
Which had been a subtle message
That Lee should toe the line.

When Kim asked Lee what just occurred
Lee had refused to say.
It's safer for the family
If they just walked away.

While some agents had been shaken
When they had re-emerged.
With reports that they'd heard laughter
As though their exit urged.

The laugh they claimed maniacal
Though seemed to have no source.
It truly was unsettling
As it was harsh and coarse.

Survivor's Remorse

As Lee had looked across the crowd
The grief that he had seen
Had driven spikes into his heart
Which had not been pristine.

While Lee's guilt had overwhelmed him
Where he'd come to believe
He was the one responsible
For why so many grieve.

He thought there's more he could have done
Where some he could have saved.
But he had failed in the attempt
Because his courage caved.

They had looked to him for guidance
But all his efforts failed.
He felt the need to take the blame
As on them he had bailed.

He wondered if those people knew
That he had been to blame.
But, probably, they had no clue
Nor even knew his name.

He then thought that he should tell them
In hope they'd not forgive.
For after his experience
He had no right to live.

No Confession

For Kim he had undying love
That's tainted by remorse.
Temptation was presented him
Though he'd not chose that course.

But the guilt that he was tempted
On him had heavy weighed.
While he feared that a confession
Would prove to Kim he strayed.

To Kim he'd felt he'd not confide
In fear of what she'd do.
Though nothing happened he believed
She'd not believe it true.

And he feared with a confession
Kim may not understand.
He stared into the face of death
Where Val offered a hand.

For after all that he'd been through
He'd no wish to lose Kim.
As she had been his one true love
And meant the world to him.

Yet, once he stopped to think of it,
He'd nothing to confess.
For nothing ever came of it
Though he had felt the stress.

A Damaged Soul

The trauma Lee experienced
Left him a damaged soul.
For Kim had seen a change in him
That she could not console.

There's no way she could imagine
The horror he'd been through.
Though something he'd internalized
Where guilt he thought he's due.

He'd found it difficult to sleep
As nightmares ruled the night.
Where images came flooding back
That he'd no will to fight.

Lee never mentioned Val to Kim
As he'd not seen the need.
She was a figure from his past
That he would not concede.

Though Lee had been affectionate
Kim felt it was restrained.
There's something Lee had kept from her
Yet, she had not complained.

Kim had feared she may have lost him
But she'd not known to who.
There was a secret that Lee kept
She was not privy to.

Though Kimberly had sought the truth
Lee had refused to say
What happened in the Labyrinth
That haunted him this way.

The damage that was done to Lee
Had clearly left him scarred.
He once was a productive man
Whose life, now, clearly marred.

Kim's only hope that given time
Their lives they could reclaim.
Where he'd, again, confide in her
And offer her a name.

The Truth Behind the Challenge

While the bodies they extracted
Had took more than a day.
The crowd refused to be disbursed
Nor could be chased away.

Its agents said that circumstance
Was what caused the delay.
Though circumstance went unexplained
Which always seemed its way.

Kim found suspicions were confirmed
As the show she had seen
Did not reflect reality
As there was no death scene.

The government had edited
What the public could view
But what the public did not know
Could rip the land in two.

There were no limits to its greed
As it clamored for more.
Its agents lived in luxury
At expense of the poor.

For the true tapes of the Challenge
The government had sold
To someone undesirable
Who paid for them with gold.

Epilog

The government called it a shame
What had occurred to Lee.
While it promised there'd be changes,
They never came to be.

There had been questions that were asked
The government ignored.
The number of claimed accidents
Had left the masses floored.

It was not held accountable
For all that had transpired.
What purpose served the Labyrinth
Where so many expired?

The prize not even half as much
As government had claimed.
Because it placed a tax on it
With more than half reclaimed.

Lee's family no better off
Than when it all began.
They still had lived in poverty
As though that was the plan.

What purpose had the Labyrinth
That it saw fit to build?
For no good seemed to come from it
With what it came to y eld.

The government had regretted
Whatever had occurred.
But it claimed it had no knowledge
While questions it deferred.

The government had been surprised
As backlash it thought queer.
With panel already planning
A Challenge for next year.

About the Author

Gordon Bostic was born in West Virginia and grew up in Virginia. A graduate of James Madison University and Fairleigh Dickinson University, he worked as a computer scientist and a software engineer for most of his life. He began writing at a young age as a way of expressing himself, his feelings and his view of the world. Gordon has also had an interest in telling his stories in one way or another. "The Walk" is his sixth novel. Gordon currently lives on the Jersey Shore with his wife, Susan.